HOW CAN BEGINNERS INVEST

Copyright pharm HaliruUK

Table of content

Chapter One
- Investments for Beginners

Chapter Two
- short-term investment

Chapter three
- How to Invest 100 Dollars

Chapter Four
- How Stock Trading Works

Chapter Five
- The Secret Power of the Stock Market

CHAPTER ONE

The greatest misinterpretation about financial planning is that it's held for the rich. That might've been valid before. In any case, that obstruction to passage is gone today, wrecked by organizations and administrations that have made it their central goal to make speculation choices accessible for everybody, including amateurs and the people who have quite recently modest quantities of cash to give something to do.

As a matter of fact, with such countless speculations now accessible to fledglings, there's not a good reason to jump out. What's more, that is uplifting news, since effective financial planning is an extraordinary method for developing your riches.

Why is effective money management significant?

You could have heard somebody think back about how modest gas costs (or another item or administration) used to be once upon a time. This is because expansion dissolves the worth of cash as years go by. By financial planning, you can all the more likely battle expansion, expanding your possibilities by having the option to manage the cost of the very measure of labour and products later on that you can today. Contributing assists you with bringing in your cash work for you gave compounding. Compound income implies that any profits you procure are reinvested to acquire unexpected returns. Furthermore, the previous you begin effective financial planning, the more advantage you gain from compounding.

What novices ought to consider
Before you hop in, there are things to ponder.
Your objectives and time skyline
Consider what objective you are needing to accomplish by money management and your time skyline, the time allotment you

need to contribute before arriving at that objective. If the time skyline to your objective is short, contributing probably won't be the best answer for you. Look at our article on the best way to contribute to present moment or long haul objectives.
Risk resilience and broadening
All speculations have some degree of hazard and the market is unpredictable, it goes all over the long run. You actually should figure out your gamble resilience. This implies measuring how agreeable you are with chance or how much instability you can deal with.
While effective money management, a decent guideline isn't to tied up your resources in one place. All things considered, expand. By spreading your dollars across different speculations, you can lessen venture risk. For this reason the speculations we frame underneath utilize common assets or trade exchanged assets generally, which permits financial backers to

buy bins of protections rather than individual stocks and bonds.

6 ventures for amateurs
The following are six ventures that are appropriate for amateur financial backers.
401(k) or manager retirement plan
A robot-consultant
Deadline shared store
File reserves
Trade exchanged reserves (ETFs)
Speculation applications

1. A 401(k) or other boss retirement plan
If you have a 401(k) or another retirement plan at work, it's probable the primary spot you ought to put your cash — particularly assuming your organization matches a piece of your commitments. That match is free cash and a dependable profit from your venture.
You can begin with just 1% of every check, however, it's smart to hold back nothing least how much your manager match. For

instance, a typical matching plan is half of the first 6% of the compensation you contribute. To catch the full match in that situation, you would need to contribute 6% of your compensation every year. Yet, you can move gradually up to that after some time.

At the point when you choose to add to a 401(k), the cash will go straightforwardly from your check into the record while never coming to your bank. Generally, 401(k) commitments are made pretax. Some 401(k)s today will put your assets naturally in a deadline reserve — more on those underneath — yet you might have different options. This is the way to put resources into your 401(k).

To pursue your 401(k) or become familiar with your particular arrangement, contact your HR office.

2. A robot-guide

Perhaps you're on this page to eat your peas, in a manner of speaking: You realize you should contribute, you've figured out how to figure out a tad of cash to do as such, yet you would prefer to disavow what is going on.

There's uplifting news: You to a great extent can, because of robot counsels. These administrations deal with your ventures for you utilizing PC calculations. Because of the low above, they charge low expenses compared with human venture chiefs — a robot guide ordinarily costs 0.25% to 0.50% of your record balance each year, and many permits you to open a record with no base. They're an extraordinary way for fledglings to begin financial planning since they frequently require next to no cash and they do the greater part of the work for you. Saying this doesn't imply that you shouldn't keep your eyes on yourself — this is your cash; you never need to be uninvolved — yet a robot counsellor will do the hard work. Furthermore, on the off chance that you're keen on figuring out how to contribute, yet you want a little assistance finding a workable pace, robot counsels can help there, as well. It's valuable to perceive how the help builds a portfolio and what ventures are utilized. A few administrations likewise offer instructive substance and devices, and a couple even permits you to modify your portfolio to some extent on the off chance that you wish to try a piece from here on out.

» Need assistance contributing? Find out about robot-counsels

3. Deadline common assets

These are similar to the robot-counsellor from past times, however, they're still broadly utilized and unimaginably famous, particularly in boss retirement plans. Deadline shared reserves are retirement speculations that consequently put considering your assessed retirement year. We should back up a bit and make sense of what a common asset is: basically, a bushel of ventures. Financial backers purchase an offer in the asset and in doing as such, they put resources into the asset's all's possessions with one exchange.

An expert chief normally picks how the asset is contributed, yet there will be a general subject of some sort: For instance, a U.S. value common asset will put resources into U.S. stocks (additionally called values).

A deadline common asset frequently holds a blend of stocks and bonds. If you intend to resign in 30 years, you could pick a deadline reserve with 2050 or 2055 in the name. That asset will at first hold generally stocks since your retirement date is far away, and stock returns will quite often be higher over the long haul.

Over the long run, it will gradually move a portion of your cash toward bonds, keeping the basic rule that you need to face a piece less challenge as you approach retirement.

4. List reserves

Record reserves resemble shared assets on autopilot: Rather than utilizing an expert supervisor to construct and keep up with the asset's arrangement of speculations, file subsidizes track a market list.

A market record is a determination of ventures that address a piece of the market. For instance, the S&P 500 is a market file that holds the supplies of about 500 of the biggest organizations in the U.S. A S&P 500 file asset would expect to reflect the exhibition of the S&P 500, purchasing the stocks in that list.

Since file supports adopt an uninvolved strategy to financial planning by following a market record instead of utilizing a proficient portfolio the executives will generally convey lower cost proportions — an expense charged in light of the sum you have contributed — than shared reserves. Be that as it may, as common assets, financial backers in file reserves are purchasing a lump of the market in one exchange.

List assets can have the least speculation prerequisites, yet some financier firms, including Fidelity and Charles Schwab, offer a choice of record assets with no base. That implies you can start putting resources into a file reserve for under $100.

5. Trade exchanged reserves (ETFs)
ETFs work in a considerable lot of the same ways as record reserves: They ordinarily track a market file and adopt a latent strategy for money management. They additionally will quite often have lower expenses than common assets. Very much like a record store, you can purchase an ETF that tracks a market file like the S&P 500.
The fundamental contrast between ETFs and record reserves is that as opposed to conveying a base venture, ETFs are exchanged over the day and financial backers get them for an offer cost, which like a stock cost, can vary. That offer cost is the ETF's speculation least, and contingent upon the asset, it can go from under $100 to $300 or more.
Since ETFs are exchanged like stocks, intermediaries are used to charging a

commission to trade them. The uplifting news: Most representatives, remembering the ones for this rundown of the best ETF specialists, have dropped exchanging expenses to $0 for ETFs. If you plan to consistently put resources into an ETF — as numerous financial backers do, by making programmed speculations every month or week — you ought to pick a without commission ETF so you're not paying a commission each time.

6. Speculation applications
A few financial planning applications target novice financial backers.
One is Acorns, which gathers together your buys on connected charge or Visas and puts the adjustment of a broadened arrangement of ETFs. On that end, it works like a robot counsel, dealing with that portfolio for you. There is no base to open an Acorns account, and the help will begin effective financial planning for you whenever you've aggregated somewhere around $5 in

round-ups. You can likewise set aside singular amount instalments.
Another application choice is Stash, which helps show novice financial backers how to fabricate their portfolios out of ETFs and individual stocks. Stash likewise offers an oversaw portfolio.

If you are prepared to begin putting resources into the financial exchange but aren't certain of the first moves toward taking while putting resources into quite a while, you've come to the ideal location.

It could shock you to discover that a $10,000 interest in the S&P 500 list a long time back would be worth almost $1.2 million today. Stock money management, when gotten along nicely, is among the best ways of creating long-haul financial momentum. We are here to show you the ropes.

There's a lot you ought to be aware of before you make a plunge. Here is a bit-by-bit manual for putting cash in the financial exchange to assist with guaranteeing you're doing it the correct way.

5 Steps to Start Investing
1. Decide your money management approach
The primary thing to consider is how to begin putting resources into stocks. A few financial backers decide to purchase individual stocks, while others adopt a less dynamic strategy.

Attempt this. Which of the accompanying statement

I'm a logical individual and appreciate doing the math and investigating.
I disdain math and don't have any desire to do a lot of "schoolwork."

I have a few hours every week to devote to financial exchange and effective money management.
I like to learn about the various organizations I can put resources into, however, want to plunge into anything math-related.
I'm a bustling proficient and lack the opportunity and energy to figure out how to examine stocks.
Fortunately paying little heed to which of these assertions you concur with, you're as yet an extraordinary possibility to turn into a financial exchange financial backer. The main thing that will change is the "how."

The various ways of putting resources into the securities exchange
Individual stocks: You can put resources into individual stocks if - - and provided that - - you have the opportunity and want to explore and assess stocks on a continuous premise completely. If so, we 100 per cent urge you to do as such. It is not too difficult

to imagine for a shrewd and patient financial backer to beat the market over the long run. Then again, on the off chance that things like quarterly profit reports and moderate numerical estimations don't sound engaging, adopting a more inactive strategy checks out.

Record assets: as well as purchasing individual stocks, you can decide to put resources into file reserves, which track a stock record like the S&P 500. With regards to effectively versus latently oversaw reserves, we for the most part favour the last option (even though there are unquestionably special cases). Record reserves normally have essentially lower costs and are practically ensured to match the drawn-out presentation of their hidden files. Over the long haul, the S&P 500 has created absolute returns of around 10% annualized, and execution like this can create significant financial wellbeing over the long run.

Robo-counselors: Finally, one more choice that has detonated in prominence as of late is the robot-consultant. A robot consultant is a business that puts your cash for your benefit in an arrangement of record subsidies that is suitable for your age, risk resilience, and contributing objectives. Not exclusively can a robot counsellor select your speculations, yet many will upgrade your expense proficiency and make changes after some time naturally.

2. Conclude the amount you will put resources into stocks

In the first place, how about we discuss the cash you shouldn't put resources into stocks. The securities exchange is a bad situation for cash that you could require inside the following five years, at least.

While the securities exchange will more likely than not ascent over an extended time, there's a lot of vulnerability in stock costs temporarily - - truth be told, a drop of

20% at whatever year is generally typical. In 2020, during the COVID-19 pandemic, the market plunged by over 40% and bounced back to an untouched high within a couple of months.

Your just-in-case account
The cash you'll have to make your youngster's next educational cost instalment
The following year's get-away asset
The cash you're storing for an upfront instalment, regardless of whether you won't be ready to purchase a permanent place to stay for quite a long time
Resource distribution
Presently we should discuss how to manage your investable cash -- that is, the cash you won't almost certainly require inside the following five years. This is an idea known as resource distribution, and a couple of variables become an integral factor here. Your age is a significant thought, as are your specific gamble resilience and speculation goals.

How about we start with your age. The overall thought is that as you age, stocks bit by bit become a less helpful spot to keep your cash. If you're youthful, you have a long time in front of you to brave any promising and less promising times on the lookout, however, this isn't true assuming that you're resigned and dependent on your venture pay.

Here is a speedy guideline that can assist you with laying out a ballpark resource designation. Take your age and deduct it from 110. This is the rough level of your investable cash that ought to be in stocks (this incorporates shared assets and ETFs that are stock-based). The rest be in fixed-pay speculations like securities or high-return CDs. You can then change this proportion up or down contingent upon your specific gamble resistance.

For instance, suppose that you are 40 years of age. This standard recommends that 70% of your investable cash ought to be in stocks, with the other 30% in fixed pay. If you're to a greater extent a daring person or are wanting to work past the normal retirement age, you might need to move this proportion for stocks. Then again, on the off chance that you could do without large vacillations in your portfolio, you should adjust it in the other heading.

3. Open a venture account
All of the guidance about putting resources into stocks for amateurs doesn't generally help you definitely on the off chance that you have no approach to purchase stocks. To do this, you'll require a particular kind of record called an investment fund.

These records are presented by organizations like TD Ameritrade, E*Trade, Charles Schwab, and numerous others. What's more, opening a money market fund is normally a no-fuss cycle that requires just minutes. You can without much of a stretch asset your investment fund by utilizing EFT move, via mailing a check, or by wiring cash.

4. Pick your stocks

Now that we've addressed the subject of how you purchase stock, assuming you're searching for some incredible fledgling accommodating venture thoughts, the following are five extraordinary stocks to assist with kicking you off.

Obviously, in only a couple of passages we can't go over all that you ought to consider while choosing and dissecting stocks, yet here are the significant ideas to dominate before you get everything rolling:

Expand your portfolio.
Put exclusively in organizations you get it.

Stay away from high-unpredictability stocks until you get the hang of money management.

Continuously stay away from penny stocks. Become familiar with the fundamental measurements and ideas for assessing stocks.

It's really smart to become familiar with the idea of enhancement, implying that you ought to have a wide range of kinds of organizations in your portfolio. In any case, I'd alert against a lot of enhancement. Stay with organizations you get it - - and assuming that incidentally, you're great at (or OK with) assessing a specific sort of stock, nothing bad can be said about one industry making up a generally enormous fragment of your portfolio.

Purchasing conspicuous high-development stocks might appear to be an incredible method for creating financial stability (and it surely can be), however, I'd alert you to hold off on these until you're somewhat more experienced. It's more shrewd to make a "base" to your portfolio with unshakable, laid-out organizations.

To put resources into individual stocks, you ought to get to know a portion of the essential ways of assessing them. Our manual for esteem effective money management is an extraordinary spot to begin. There we assist you with finding stocks exchanging for alluring valuations. What's more, if you need to add some thrilling long-haul development possibilities to your portfolio, our manual for development contributing is an incredible spot to start.

5. Contribute
Here's one of the greatest privileged insights of effective money management, the graciousness of the Oracle of Omaha himself, Warren Buffett. You don't have to do unprecedented things to obtain remarkable outcomes. (Note: Warren Buffett

isn't just the best long-haul financial backer ever, yet, in addition, one of the most amazing wellsprings of astuteness for your speculation procedure.)

The most reliable method for bringing in cash in the financial exchange is to purchase portions of extraordinary organizations at sensible costs and clutch the offers however long the organizations stay perfect (or until you want the cash). Assuming you do this, you'll encounter some unpredictability en route, yet over the long run, you'll create fantastic speculation returns.

Putting resources into stocks has become progressively available, with novices ready to open a record with minimal expenditure through a financier's site or portable application.

Stock addresses a possession stake in an organization as a typical investor. Normal stocks permit investors to decide on organization issues, with most organizations allowing one vote for each offer. A few organizations likewise offer investors profit payouts, providing financial backers with a flood of pay on top of the market worth of the stock. These payouts regularly change in light of the organization's benefit.

Stocks are viewed as a gambling resource that can give development and pay to a speculation portfolio. This implies it's a resource class that conveys a serious level of cost unpredictability. With stocks, fledgling financial backers should think about the level of chance that they can take. Ordinarily, the more gambling in speculation, the more prominent the possible prize. Be that as it may, financial backers should face the challenge of losing cash on the off chance that exceptional yields don't come. History shows that stocks have been a dependable resource class with major areas of strength for normal returns over the long run.

This is what else you want to realize about putting resources into stocks:

Where to begin putting resources into stocks.
How much cash would it be advisable for you to begin putting resources into the securities exchange?
Have an effective money management procedure, particularly during market instability.
Instructions to pick which speculations to make.
Contribute all alone or with a monetary counsellor?
Stocks for fledgling financial backers.
Use mitigating risk over the long term.
When to sell a stock.
Where to Start Investing in Stocks

The initial step is for you to open a money market fund. You want this record to get to interests in the securities exchange.

The subsequent stage is to finance your investment fund by moving cash from your financial balance to fill exchanges of stocks you need to purchase. How much cash you decide to contribute relies upon your gamble resistance, objectives and how much cash you're agreeable possibly losing.

Recollect that while, over the long haul, the securities exchange normally increments in esteem, there can be transient market vacillations, which can jeopardize your cash.

The amount of Money Should You Start Investing in the Stock Market?

A few internet-based intermediaries, for example, Betterment don't charge expenses for a $0 account surplus, nor do they require a base add up to open an exchanging account. You can begin effective financial planning through these businesses with any sum. A few likewise offer fragmentary offers, meaning you don't need to purchase a whole portion of an organization on the off chance that you can't manage the cost of it.

Markdown dealers help fledglings with minimal expenditure who are in many cases hoping to get financial exchange openness with more modest portfolios. Yet, a markdown dealer normally doesn't give guidance or investigation. Large numbers of these representatives don't need a base add-up to begin a record, while some have a low starting limit of $1,000.

Have an Investing Strategy, Especially During Market Volatility

It is typical for the securities exchange to encounter episodes of instability. During those periods, stocks, even ones considered moderately protected, experience cost vacillations. This can happen when there is a vulnerability in the business sectors and will in general be fleeting.

"By and large)," says Daniel Beckerman, leader of Beckerman Institutional in Ocean Grove, New Jersey. You ought to plan to be contributed during these unpleasant periods, Beckerman says, on the off chance that you hope to do well all through your venture time skyline.

Unpredictability can positively be unsettling, particularly if you are a novice who hasn't encountered it previously. All things considered, you ought to place your cash in organizations that can produce reliably developing income and benefit over a significant stretch. Like that, you believe in the organization notwithstanding the stock's cost swings.

"We consider an organization's capacity to battle off rivalry," Beckerman says. "If an organization is difficult to rival, they will be less inclined to run into issues with falling income and benefits from now on. They are likewise bound to be in a situation to have the option to bring their costs up in an inflationary climate, as we have encountered."

He additionally noticed that unpredictability can be your companion. Bear markets, similar to the one that has tormented the business sectors in the principal half of 2022, can be extraordinary purchasing open doors.

"The precarious part is that we don't have a clue about the date that a bear market will end," Beckerman says. "Notwithstanding, on the off chance that we take a normal of the past 10 bear showcases, the securities exchange will, in general, give positive returns of more than 14% a year after having entered the bear market."

At the point when financial backers have conviction in an organization and its stock cost falls, they might consider this to be a potential chance to purchase a greater amount of the stock at a superior cost.

Step-by-step instructions to Choose Which Investments to Make

Beckerman expresses that by taking a gander at an organization's measurements, you can acquire an understanding of how organizations and ventures are performing.

"For instance, when value profit or cost deals proportions are raised, we can get some sense regarding when certain stocks or enterprises are evaluated in bubble an area," he says. "This was the situation in 2021 when numerous unrewarding innovation stocks were exchanging what I would consider an exaggerated area."

Valuation is a significant element while stock picking. Organization benefit, income development possibilities, nature of the board and industry execution are a few variables financial backers should consider while assessing a stock's worth to decide if it is underestimated or exaggerated. According to stock valuations, Beckerman gives financial backers some variety around the opinion in regards to different industry gatherings.

A stock's cost can be not the same as its natural worth. To know how to esteem a stock, financial backers should dive into the organization's monetary detailing history, comprehend the organization's part in its industry and the way that it passages among its rivals, among numerous different variables.

"Keep away from stocks that are theoretical in nature with no verifiable presentation on the development and the board skill," says Alex Vela, a portfolio director at FBB Capital Partners. He says to target organizations with essentially a five-year history, and a supervisory crew that has clear objectives and goals.

"Similarly significant is assuming administration is carrying out any ESG strategies that lead to socially supportable strategic approaches," he expresses, alluding to natural, social and administration drives.

There are two methods for getting benefits from stock financial planning: selling shares when their reasonable worth goes up and profit instalments. Profits are instalments in one or the other money or stock made by the organization to the investor on a month-to-month, quarterly or yearly premise. Profit instalments are a way a public corporation imparts its abundance to its financial backers. Financial backers who need a constant flow of pay from their stock portfolios put resources into organizations that share their benefits as profits.

Contribute all alone or With a Financial Advisor?

Putting resources into stocks should be possible in numerous ways, yet before you begin effective financial planning, it's vital to figure out what kind of financial backer you are. Conclude whether you need to adopt a DIY strategy or work with an expert monetary counsellor who can prompt you through your abundance the board.

Burglarize Burnette, CEO, monetary consultant and expert expense preparer at Outlook Financial Center, says to pose yourself two inquiries: "First, how long and assets would you say you will focus on expressly dealing with your records?

Second, how persistent will you be in regards to getting at first taught and proceeding with that schooling forever?"

To adopt the DIY strategy and deal with your ventures, you can open an internet-based investment fund. On the off chance that you're uncertain about where to begin, consider opening a record with a robot counsellor, which will do a portion of the hard work at a lower cost.

"Most counsellors won't work with little records even though there isn't anything possibly better than talking with a guide that is a guardian," Burnette says. "The exhortation can be more engaged, and you can find direct solutions to coordinate inquiries instead of depending on the individual that gets the telephone at a call place."

He says starting financial backers might have the option to track down a trustee counsel with low or no record essentials.

When you open a web-based money market fund, you're posed inquiries to decide on a venture technique that will aid your speculation choices. These inquiries include knowing your particular monetary objectives - like retirement or a major buy - and your gamble resilience, which is the level of market fluctuation you can endure in your speculations.

Characterize your objectives before you begin effective money management. These will drive your dynamic cycles.

For instance, assuming that exit from the workforce is your objective, you might need to slant your portfolio toward more development situated interests with an end goal to produce the best yield conceivable. However, assuming that you're pursuing an objective that is nearer within reach, for example, purchasing your most memorable house, you'd be in an ideal situation with a more safe portfolio so you don't risk your speculations losing esteem when now is the right time to make the buy.

On the off chance that you don't know how to emerge you are drawn out monetary objectives and where to begin with your effective money management plan, working with a monetary guide might be ideal for you.

"Many individuals decide to employ somebody who has practical experience in the field so they can exploit their mastery thus they don't have to stress over the things they might miss or that they don't have any idea," says Jeffrey Wood, a speculation counsellor and accomplice at Lift Financial. "It likewise assists with having a believed guide that you can call with various forms of feedback."

Monetary counsellors can safeguard you from settling on choices that may not benefit you. If you have any desire to purchase individual stocks, you should comprehend that they can convey substantially more gamble than different protections, for example, common assets or trade exchanged reserves. All things considered, on the off chance that you don't know the amount of your cash you ought to distribute toward stocks, you can work with a monetary counsellor to foster a system.

Monetary consultants can assist with different areas of monetary preparation, as well, for example, school arranging, duty and bequest arranging, resource security and aiding friends and family, Beckerman says. "We are finding that financial backers who began with an internet-based stage are relocating to us once their necessities become more complex."

Stocks for Beginner Investors

Figuring you can reliably beat the market can be a waste of time, yet putting resources into top-notch stocks, for example, blue chips and profit-yielding organizations is in many cases a decent procedure for fledglings.

One explanation financial backers decide on blue chips is their history of dependability and because they will generally deliver profits. Popular blue-chip organizations incorporate Microsoft, Coca-Cola Co. (KO) and Procter and Gamble Co. (PG). Coca-Cola, for instance, produces a profit yield of practically 2.8% - meaning a financial backer would procure 2.8% of their speculation level in profits throughout the following year at the ongoing profit rate - and the stock is less unpredictable, as its portion cost has floated somewhere in the range of $52 and $67 during the beyond 52 weeks as of mid-July. Profits can produce truly necessary pay for financial backers.

Long haul financial backers who exploit a purchase and-hold technique by going long on stocks can receive the rewards of long haul development in market esteem. For instance, assuming you purchased portions of AT&T Inc. (T) at its first sale of stock cost of $1.25 in 1984, your venture would be worth undeniably more than whatever you put in, as the stock presently exchanges at about $20 per share and has been delivering profits for quite a long time.

Use Dollar-Cost Averaging

After picking what stocks to purchase, the inquiry becomes when to get them. The familiar saying "purchase low, sell high," is a decent one to follow, however, it's difficult to tell when a stock is at a low.

To mitigate the inclination that you should time the market perfectly, many starting financial backers benefit from a minimizing risk methodology by which you contribute a decent sum on a standard timetable, no matter what the stock's ongoing cost.

"Many starting financial backers might get disappointed with the everyday vacillations and ups-and-downs of the securities exchange, yet minimizing risk over the long haul in a fluctuating — however by and large up-moving — market permits a financial backer to persistently contribute and purchase more offers when the market plunges, making their general expense premise normal lower overall than their sell esteem," Wood says. "Markets are challenging to time, yet mitigating risk assists with making investment funds propensities that, over the long run, have displayed to generally achieve positive outcomes."

All things considered, a few financial backers improve money management by a single amount at the same time. This can help you out because it's for the most part better to put away cash sooner as opposed to sitting on cash.

"Either minimizing risk or lump putting when utilized in longer, long term money management techniques will, in general, allow a financial backer a superior opportunity of positive speculation returns than when utilized during momentary periods," Wood says.

When to Sell a Stock

Knowing when to let a stock go - without choosing in a frenzy - is vital expertise for keen financial backers.

Burnette says the most effective recommendation he got from a Wall Street billion-dollar cash chief was to "characterize the exit before you get in."

"For instance, set a metric that expects you to return to a stock when it is up 20% or down 10%," he says. At the point when your measurement is set off, ask yourself: "Is this still a wise speculation?" Doing so drives you to take a gander at the stock's honest evaluation and the organization's ongoing standing.

Having a leave plan set up will assist you with keeping feelings out of the choice of when to sell. It's significant not to go gaga for the stock since organizations change and organizations can fizzle.

Following the consistent pattern of media reporting that encompasses an organization's stock exhibition can overpower. All things considered, specialists say to overlook the momentary clamour, so you can keep up with the viewpoint inside your methodology for the long run.

At the point when it comes time to sell, remember to think about the assessment suggestions. "Assuming you hold a venture for more than a one-year time frame before selling, charges on the enthusiasm for that stock will be charged at a lower long haul capital increases rate as opposed to a higher momentary capital increases charge rate for speculations held short of what one year," Wood says.

Amazing financial backer Warren Buffett encourages individuals to purchase and hold stocks for quite some time as opposed to selling and repurchasing them continually. At any rate, an imminent stock ought to be one that a financial backer would possess for no less than 10 years, as indicated by his way of thinking.

CHAPTER TWO

If you're hoping to put away cash for the present moment, you're most likely looking for a protected spot to stash cash before you want to get to it not long from now. The unpredictable business sectors and drooping economy drove numerous financial backers to hold cash as the Covid emergency was delayed — and things stay questionable as the economy currently faces flooding expansion.

Transient ventures limit risk, yet at the expense of possibly more significant yields accessible in the best long-haul speculations. Subsequently, you'll guarantee that you have cash when you want it, rather than wasting the cash on possibly dangerous speculation. So the main thing financial backers ought to be searching for in a momentary venture is wellbeing.

What is transient speculation?

If you're making transient speculation, you're frequently doing so because you want to have the cash at a specific time. If you're putting something aside for an upfront instalment on a house or a wedding, for instance, the cash should be good to go. Momentary ventures are those you make for under three years.

On the off chance that you make some more extended memories skyline - no less than three to five years (and, surprisingly, longer is better) - you can see ventures like stocks. Stocks offer the potential for a lot better yields. The financial exchange has generally risen a normal of 10% yearly over extensive stretches - yet it has demonstrated to be very unstable. So the more extended time skyline empowers you to brave the promising and less promising times of the securities exchange.

Transient ventures: Safe however lower yield

The well-being of transient speculations includes some significant pitfalls. You probably will not have the option to procure as much in transient speculation as you would in a drawn-out venture. If you contribute for the present moment, you'll be restricted to particular sorts of speculations and shouldn't buy less secure resources like stocks and stock assets. (In any case, on the off chance that you can contribute as long as possible, this is the way to purchase stocks.)

Transient speculations do have two or three benefits, nonetheless. They're much of the time profoundly fluid, so you can get your cash at whatever point you want it. Likewise, they will generally be lower risk than long-haul ventures, so you might have restricted drawbacks or even none by any stretch of the imagination.

The following are a couple of the best momentary speculations to consider that offer you some return.

1. High return investment accounts

A high-return investment account at a bank or credit association is a decent option in contrast to holding cash in a financial record, which regularly pays next to no premium on your store. The bank will pay revenue in a bank account consistently.

Savers would do well to correlation shop high return investment accounts since it's not difficult to track down which banks offer the most elevated loan fees and they are not difficult to set up.

Risk: Savings accounts are guaranteed by the Federal Deposit Insurance Corporation (FDIC) at banks and by the National Credit Union Administration (NCUA) at credit associations, so you will not lose cash. There's not exactly a gamble to these records for the time being, however financial backers who hold their cash over longer periods might experience difficulty staying aware of expansion.

Liquidity: Savings accounts are exceptionally fluid, and you can add cash to the record. Bank accounts commonly just take into consideration up to six expense-free withdrawals or moves per articulation cycle, nonetheless. (The Federal Reserve presently permits banks to postpone this prerequisite.) you'll need to look out for banks that charge expenses for keeping up with the record or getting to ATMs, so you can limit those.

2. Transient corporate security reserves

Corporate securities are securities given by large companies to subsidize their ventures. They are normally viewed as protected and pay interest at customary spans, maybe quarterly or two times per year.

Security reserves are assortments of these corporate securities from a wide range of organizations, normally across numerous ventures and company sizes. This enhancement implies that an ineffectively performing bond won't hurt the general return without a doubt. The security asset will pay interest consistently, commonly month to month.

Risk: A momentary corporate security reserve isn't protected by the public authority, so it can lose cash. Notwithstanding, bonds will generally be very protected, particularly if you're purchasing an extensively expanded assortment of them. Likewise, a transient asset gives the minimal measure of hazard openness to changing financing costs, so increasing or falling rates won't influence the cost of the asset to an extreme.

Liquidity: A momentary corporate security store is profoundly fluid, and it tends to be traded on any day that the monetary business sectors are open.

3. Currency market accounts

Currency market accounts are one more sort of bank store, and they ordinarily pay a higher financing cost than normal investment accounts, however, they regularly require a higher least venture, as well.

Risk: Be certain to find a currency market account that is FDIC-guaranteed so your record will be shielded from losing cash, with inclusion up to $250,000 per investor, per bank.

Like a bank account, the significant gamble for currency market accounts happens after some time, because their low loan fees typically make it challenging for financial backers to stay aware of expansion. For the time being, in any case, that is not a critical concern.

Liquidity: Money market accounts are exceptionally fluid, however, government regulations do force a few limitations on withdrawals.

4. Cash the executive's accounts

The money executive's account permits you to place cash in different momentary ventures, and it acts similar to an omnibus record. You can frequently contribute, discount takes a look at the record, move cash and do other commonplace bank-like exercises. Cash the executive's accounts are regularly presented by robot consultants and online stock intermediaries.

So the money the board account provides you with a ton of adaptability.

Risk: Cash the executive's accounts are many times put resources into safe low-yield currency market reserves, so there's not much of hazard. On account of some robot-counsellor accounts, these foundations store your cash into FDIC-safeguarded accomplice banks, so you should ensure that you don't surpass FDIC store inclusion assuming you as of now work with one of the accomplice banks.

Liquidity: Cash the board accounts are incredibly fluid, and cash can be removed whenever. In this regard, they might be far superior to conventional reserve funds and currency market accounts, which limit month-to-month withdrawals.

6. No-punishment authentications of store

A no-punishment testament of the store, or CD, allows you to evade the regular expense that the bank charges on the off chance that you drop your CD before it develops. You can track down CDs at your bank, and they'll commonly offer a better yield than you could find in other bank items, for example, investment accounts and currency market accounts.

Discs are time stores, meaning when you open one, you're consenting to hold the cash in the record for a predefined timeframe, going from times of weeks up to numerous years, contingent upon the development you need. In return for the security of having this cash in its vault, the bank will pay you a higher financing cost.

The bank pays revenue on the CD routinely, and toward the finish of the CD's expression, the bank will return your essentials in addition to the procured revenue.

A no-punishment CD may likewise be alluring in a time of increasing loan costs since you can pull out your cash without paying an expense and afterwards store it somewhere else for a better yield.

Risk: CDs are protected by the FDIC, so you will not lose any cash on them. The dangers are restricted for a transient CD, however, one gamble is that you might pass up a superior rate somewhere else while your cash is restricted in the CD. Assuming the loan fee is excessively low, you may likewise wind up losing buying capacity to expand.

Liquidity: CDs are ordinarily less fluid than other bank ventures on this rundown, yet a no-punishment CD permits you to stay away from the charge for finishing the CD early. So you can avoid the key component that makes most CDs illiquid.

7. Treasurys

Treasurys come in three assortments - T-charges, T-securities and T-notes - and they offer a definitive safe yield, supported by the AAA credit score of the U.S. national government. So instead of purchasing an administration security reserve, you could select to purchase explicit protections, contingent upon your necessities.

Risk: As with a security reserve, individual securities are not supported by the FDIC, but rather are upheld by the public authority's guarantee to reimburse the cash, so they're viewed as exceptionally protected.

Liquidity: U.S. government securities are the most fluid securities on the trades, and can be traded on any day the market is open.

8. Currency market common assets

Try not to befuddle a currency market shared reserve with a currency market account. While they're named in basically the same manner, they have various dangers, however, both are great transient speculations. A currency market shared store puts resources into transient protections, including Treasurys, civil and corporate obligations, as well as bank obligation protections. What's more, since it's a common asset, you'll pay a cost proportional to the asset organization from the resources being made due.

Risk: While its ventures are by and large protected, currency market reserves are not so protected as currency market accounts, which are FDIC-supported. Conversely, currency market assets can lose cash, commonly just in times of serious market trouble, yet they are for the most part very protected. In any case, they are probably the safest speculations accessible and ought to safeguard your cash.

Liquidity: Money market common assets are sensibly fluid, and you can get to your cash promptly. They might permit you to discount taking a look at the asset, however, you're commonly restricted to six withdrawals each month.

What makes a decent momentary venture?

Great transient speculations might share numerous things for all intents and purposes, yet they are normally portrayed by the accompanying three attributes:

Dependability: Good transient speculations don't vary a lot in esteem, as many stocks and bonds do. The cash will be there when you want it and is frequently safeguarded by FDIC protection or an administration ensure. Liquidity: A decent transient speculation normally offers high liquidity, implying that you can get to the money and put resources into it rapidly. On account of specific CDs, you'll know when the cash opens up, and you can continuously reclaim the CD, however, it will frequently accompany a punishment, except if you decide on a no-punishment CD.

Low exchange costs: A decent transient speculation doesn't cost a huge load of cash to get into or out of, in contrast to a house, for instance. That is particularly significant when yields on transient ventures are at authentic lows.

These elements imply that your cash won't be in danger and will be open when you want to utilize it, which is one of the significant motivations to have transient speculation. Interestingly, you can procure a better yield on long-haul ventures yet should get through more momentary instability. Assuming that you want that cash, however, you could need to completely get rid of it at an inopportune time to get to it.

Ways to put away cash for quite a long time or less

On the off chance that you're putting away cash for quite some time or less, you ought to have an unexpected cycle in comparison to assuming you were financial planning with a period skyline of many years. All things being equal, you want to move toward transient financial planning with the accompanying tips:

Set your assumptions. Momentary ventures will have lower likely returns than long-haul speculations, so it's critical to suitably set your assumptions.
Center around wellbeing. As a rule, if you're effective money management for the present moment, you ought to zero in on security as opposed to return. Your cash ought to be there when you want it.
Some additional returns may not merit the additional gamble. With momentary ventures procuring nearly nothing, it tends to be not difficult to attempt to get some additional return to the detriment of significantly more gambling. Be that as it

may, centre around why you're money management for the present moment. Pick the speculation given your requirements. You could procure some extra on that CD, however, imagine a scenario where you want to get to the cash before it develops. Align your venture type to your necessities.

Not all transient speculations are equivalent. Bank items are supported by the FDIC, so you will not lose any head. Yet, market-based items, even safe ones like transient security reserves, could decline over brief periods. Figure out the dangers of your speculations.

Momentary speculations are typically protected, particularly compared with longer-term ventures like stocks or stock assets. Yet, be certain you comprehend what you're putting resources into.

CHAPTER THREE

You can create genuinely financial well-being beginning with a little amount of cash, and without succumbing to make easy money tricks.

Contributing can completely change yourself to improve things. Yet, many individuals erroneously imagine that except if they have a huge number of dollars lying around, there's no decent spot to put their cash. Fortunately essentially not the situation. You can begin effective financial planning with $100 or even less.

The main thing - - and how you can get those bigger aggregates - - is to simply get everything rolling, regardless of how enormous or little, your speculation dollars are toward the start. In this article, you'll find out around six extraordinary ways of effective money management two or three hundred bucks. By placing your cash in at least one of these classifications given your short-and long haul objectives, you can begin money management on your way toward long-haul monetary freedom.

Our 6 most ideal ways to contribute $100 beginning today
You have $100, and you're hoping to give it something to do. Here are our six best ideas for how to manage it:

Begin a secret stash.
Utilize a miniature money management application or robot counsel.
Put resources into a stock record common asset or trade exchanged reserve.
Utilize partial offers to purchase stocks.
Put it in your 401(k).
Open an IRA.
Presently we should investigate every one of these in more detail.

1. Begin a rainy day account

It's reasonable assuming your most memorable idea was to begin by taking your $100 and purchasing stocks, digital currencies, or some other speculation that could twofold, triple, or even increment your cash 10-overlay. All things considered, the financial exchange has done right by being the least complex and most available way for individuals to create their financial momentum over the long run. Numerous digital currencies have acquired immensely esteem throughout recent years.

However, those resources are additionally unstable. They can fall in esteem pointedly with practically zero advance notice and frequently without an unmistakable justification for why. That is not any joking matter assuming that you're ready to purchase and hold, thus lengthy as you own a differentiated blend of speculations where your victors can compensate for a couple of washouts. Time in the market will assist you with making riches.

Yet, consider the possibility that you can't simply hold those speculations through an accident and need to sell since you want the cash. A little misfortune and timing could mean your $100 speculation is presently worth $80, or $50, or even less. That is the reason beginning with cash in reserve funds is undeniably more significant than picking speculations that can be truly unstable.

Suppose you were to lose your employment or experience an unforeseen sickness or mishap that impacted your pay for quite a long time or even months. Having a while of pay accessible in real money can mean holding life's surprising occasions back from harming your monetary plans. Financing costs on investment accounts aren't extremely high, however, this is tied in with safeguarding your drawback - - not catching exceptional yields.

2. Utilize a miniature money management application or robot-counsel

When you take care of monetary crises, you're in a vastly improved position to begin money management. Assuming that you like a completely mechanized approach that expects as little exertion as could be expected, then, at that point, a robot guide might be exactly the thing you're searching for. Robo-guides use applications or sites to find out about your monetary necessities and afterwards think of an effective financial planning procedure to meet them. They'll frequently utilize fundamental data, for example, age, family size, pay, and chance resilience to fit a portfolio to your necessities. Robo-counselors then, at that point, handle every one of the subtleties of choosing ventures, making buys and deals, and keeping you informed.

You could likewise utilize a miniature financial planning application, which permits financial backers to give limited quantities of cash something to do over the long run. For instance, a miniature financial planning application could permit you to gather together your Visa buys to the closest dollar and contribute the distinction while likewise permitting you to store reserves when you have additional cash (like $100) to contribute.

3. Put resources into a stock file common asset or trade exchanged store
Stocks are likely the most remarkable growing substantial financial foundation instrument that the typical individual can purchase. Be that as it may, it very well may be truly difficult to pick the victors, and, assuming you're just money management $100 (or even less) at a time, it might not merit the time and work to pick individual stocks. This is where stock record subsidies come in.

It's likewise easy to do. You just put your cash into a stock file common asset or a minimal expense trade exchanged reserve. You can browse a wide assortment of stock files, going from well-known ones like the S&P 500 Index to additional specific records.

There are a few distinctions between ETFs and common assets, including how you trade shares, what least ventures apply, and what charges you can hope to pay. In any case, the overall thought behind the two ETFs and shared reserves is that you can put resources into the entire market or in chose portions of it through solitary speculation.

Whenever you've developed a strong groundwork in these file following assets, you can stretch out and investigate other money management choices. Yet, a file asset likely could be everything you'll at any point truly need to prevail with your effective money management. Intrigued by a file reserve that costs more than $100? The following subject applies to ETFs, as well!

4. Utilize fragmentary offers to purchase stocks

File finances make stock money management simple, however, picking your stocks is an incredible method for procuring far superior returns. In any case, up to this point, the blend of business commissions and stock costs kept anybody working with more modest amounts of cash outwardly searching in.

That is not the case any longer since most specialists never again charge commissions, and a few significant businesses offer fragmentary offer money management.

So what precisely is fragmentary offer money management? So, rather than placing a request for various offers to get, you tell your representative the number of dollars you need to put resources into a stock, and your merchant will put that measure of cash in that stock for you. For instance, assuming that you put $100 in a stock that exchanged for $500, your money market fund would show that you possessed 0.2 portions of that organization.

Hoping to put resources into list reserves? Uplifting news! Most agents who offer fragmentary money management for stocks will likewise allow you to purchase partial portions of ETFs also.

5. Put it in your 401(k)
On the off chance that you have a 401(k) or another business-supported retirement plan, financing it very well may be a fantastic utilization of your venture dollars. That is particularly obvious if you haven't maximized your manager's matching commitments. What's that? It implies that most managers will match a portion of the cash you put in your 401(k).

Here is a model: Let's say your boss matches half of your commitments, up to 3% of your compensation. Assuming you acquire $50,000 each year, your boss will put $750 in your 401(k) for the first $1,500 - - 3% of your compensation - - that you contribute. That is a half increase on that $125 each month you contributed.

There's something else to like about putting resources into your 401(k): lower charges. Each dollar you add to your 401(k) is viewed as a pre-charge commitment, meaning you won't pay a personal expense on that dollar the year you contributed it to your record. Even better, your speculations will develop tax-exempt until you begin taking dispersions in retirement.

Try not to have a business, or have a second job or agreement gig? Prepare to have your mind blown. You can open a solo 401(k). You will not get the free cash from a business, yet you can in any case exploit those pre-charge commitments and tax-exempt development.

6. Open an IRA

Have an extra $100 you need to contribute for retirement far more than your organization's 401(k)? A singular retirement account (IRA) is an extraordinary approach and can transform even little amounts of cash into major savings over the long haul.

Suppose that you stash $100 a month in an IRA for a considerable length of time. Given the S&P 500's verifiable exhibition, the $36,000 you contributed would be worth almost $180,000. That is the force of intensifying additions after some time.

Why an IRA? In a word, charges. With a customary IRA, you gain comparative advantages as with a 401(k), diminishing personal duties by cutting your available pay every year you contribute while likewise developing your savings tax-exempt until you begin taking dispersions in retirement.

With a Roth IRA, you get a similar tax-exempt development similarly as with a customary IRA. However, rather than getting to bring down your available pay every year, you make commitments, and dispersions in retirement are 100 per cent tax-exempt.

One way not to contribute $100
One snare to know about is putting resources into penny stocks. Penny stocks are regularly low-evaluated loads of more modest or meagerly exchanged organizations. While it might appear to be sensible that little organizations or stocks that exchange for just pennies per offer (or even less) have the best yield potential, actually the universe of penny stocks is brimming with false organizations and siphon and-dump plans (think The Wolf of Wall Street).

To put it, assuming that you're requesting how best put $100 in penny stocks, the response is, "Don't."

CHAPTER FOUR

Stock exchanging is a type of effective financial planning that focuses on momentary benefits over long-haul gains. It very well may be dangerous to make a plunge without legitimate information.

What is stock exchanging?
Stock exchanging includes trading partakes in organizations with an end goal to bring in cash on everyday changes in cost. Dealers watch the momentary value variances of these stocks intently and afterwards attempt to purchase low and sell high.
[1]
 This momentary methodology separates stock dealers from conventional financial exchange financial backers who will more often than not be in it for the long stretch. While exchanging individual stocks can bring fast gains for the people who time the market accurately, it additionally conveys the risk of significant misfortunes. A solitary

organization's fortunes can rise more rapidly than the market overall, yet they can straightforwardly fall.

"Exchanging isn't for weak-willed," says Nathaniel Moore, a confirmed monetary organizer and an ensured realm counsel at AGAPE Planning Partners in Fresno, California. "Try not to face the challenge and put away cash if you want it."

If you do have the cash and need to pick up exchanging, online financiers have made it conceivable to exchange stocks rapidly from your PC or cell phone.

Be that as it may, before you make a plunge, you ought to ensure you know how the financial exchange functions, the best applications for exchanging stocks, and how to deal with your gamble.

Sorts of stock exchanging

There are two principal kinds of stock exchange:

Dynamic exchanging is what a financial backer who places at least 10 exchanges each month does. Commonly, they utilize a methodology that depends vigorously on timing the market, attempting to exploit transient occasions (at the organization level or given market variances) to make money in the next few weeks or months. Day exchanging is the procedure utilized by financial backers who play hot potato with stocks — purchasing, selling and shutting their places of similar stock in a solitary exchanging day, thinking often minimal about the inward functions of the fundamental organizations. (Position alludes to how much a specific stock or asset you own.) The point of the informal investor is to make a couple of bucks in the following couple of minutes, hours or days given day-to-day cost vacillations.

Instructions to exchange stocks
Assuming that you're taking a stab at stock exchanging interestingly, realize that most financial backers are best served by keeping things basic and putting resources

into an expanded blend of minimal expense file assets to accomplish — and this is critical — long-haul outperformance.

All things considered, the coordinated factors of exchanging stocks boil down to six stages:

1. Open a money market fund

Stock exchanging requires subsidizing a money market fund — a particular sort of record intended to hold speculations. If you don't as of now have a record, you can open one with a web-based specialist in no time flat. Be that as it may, simply sit back and relax, opening a record doesn't mean you're putting away your cash yet. It simply gives you the choice to do so when you're prepared.

2. Set a stock exchanging financial plan

Regardless of whether you track down the ability for exchanging stocks, dispensing over 10% of your portfolio to a singular stock can open your reserve funds to a lot of unpredictability.

"On the off chance that your cash's all are in one stock, you might lose half of it short-term," Moore says.

To contribute, he says, you could begin by saving $200 per month. At the point when you get to $1,000, you could contribute $500 of that. Consider the $500 you're not financial planning like a parachute. You probably won't require it, however, it's there assuming that you do. Other do's and don'ts include:

Contribute just how much cash you can stand to lose.

Try not to utilize cash that is reserved for a close term, must-pay costs like an upfront instalment or educational cost.

Ratchet down that 10% on the off chance that you don't yet have a solid secret stash and 10% to 15% of your pay piped into a retirement investment account.

3. Figure out how to utilize market requests and breaking point orders

When you have your money market fund and financial plan set up, you can utilize your web-based merchant's site or exchanging stage to put your stock exchanges. You'll be given a few choices for request types, which direct the way that your exchange goes through. We go through these exhaustively in our aide for how to purchase stocks, yet these are the two most normal sorts:

Market request: Buys or sells the stock ASAP at the most ideal that anyone could hope to find the cost.

Limit request: Buys or sells the stock just at or better than a particular cost you set. For a purchase request, the cutoff cost will be the most you're willing to pay and the request will go through provided that the stock's value tumbles to or underneath that sum.

4. Practice with a paper exchanging account

"Have a go at putting resources into the market without placing cash on the lookout yet to simply perceive how it functions," says Moore.

You can do that by money management your time, he says, pick a stock and screen it so that three to a half years could perceive how it performs. You can likewise get familiar with the market utilizing the paper exchanging instruments presented by numerous web-based stock representatives. Virtual exchanging with financial exchange test systems allows clients to test their exchanging discernment and develop a history before risking genuine dollars.

5. Measure your profits against a fitting benchmark
This is fundamental guidance for a wide range of financial backers — not simply dynamic ones. The real objective for picking stocks is to be in front of a benchmark list. That could be the Standard and Poor's 500 records (frequently utilized as an intermediary for "the market"), the Nasdaq composite list (for those putting principally in innovation stocks) or other more modest

files that are made out of organizations given size, industry and topography. Estimating results is critical, and if a serious financial backer can't beat the benchmark (something even ace financial backers battle to do), then it seems OK to put resources into a minimal expense file shared asset or ETF — a crate of stocks whose presentation intently lines up with that of one of the benchmark records.

6. Keep your point of view
Being an effective financial backer doesn't need finding the following incredible breakout stock before every other person. When you hear that a specific stock is ready for pop, so have a huge number of expert dealers, and the potential probably has previously been estimated in the stock. It could be past the time to make a fast circle back benefit, however that doesn't mean you're past the time for the party. Extraordinary speculations keep on conveying investors an incentive for quite a

long time, which is a decent contention for regarding dynamic money management as a side interest and not a pyramid scheme.

The most effective method to oversee stock exchange chances
Any place you fall on the financial backer dealer range, these four hints for how to exchange stocks can assist with guaranteeing you do it securely.
1. Lower risk by building positions continuously
There's compelling reason need to cannonball into the profound end with any position. Taking as much time as is needed to purchase (through minimizing risk or purchasing in thirds) diminishes financial backer openness to cost unpredictability. Moore says you can likewise investigate high-profit stocks, which pay out a part of income to financial backers, and ETFs, which permit you to spread your gamble out among numerous organizations.

2. Disregard 'hot tips'
Individuals posting in web-based stock-picking discussions and paying for supported advertisements promoting sure-thing stocks are not your companions. Generally speaking, they are important for a siphon and dump racket where obscure individuals buy containers of offers in a mostly secret, meagerly exchanged organization (frequently a penny stock) and hit the web to the publicity it up.

As accidental financial backers load up on offers and drive the cost up, the criminals take their benefits, dump their portions and send the stock pitching back to earth. Try not to assist them with filling their pockets.

3. Save great records for the IRS
If you're not utilizing a record that appreciates charges leaned toward status —, for example, a 401(k) or other work environment accounts, or a Roth or customary IRA — charges on venture gains and misfortunes can get muddled.

The IRS applies various principles and duty rates and requires the recording of various structures for various sorts of brokers. If you've sold stocks for a benefit or brought in cash from selling stocks, make a point to save some additional money for a possibly bigger than-typical expense bill. One more advantage of keeping great records is that washout speculations can be utilized to counterbalance the duties paid on pay through a slick technique called charge misfortune reaping.

Where to exchange stocks

To exchange stocks you want an intermediary, yet succumb to no expedite. Pick one with the terms and apparatuses that best line up with your financial planning style and experience. A higher need for dynamic merchants will be low commissions and quick request execution for time-touchy exchanges. See our picks for the greatest day exchanging applications to find out more.

Financial backers who are new to exchanging ought to search for a representative who can show them the secrets to success using instructive articles, online instructional exercises and in-person courses (see NerdWallet's gatherings for the best merchants for novices). Different elements to consider with stock exchanging applications are the quality and accessibility of screening and stock investigation apparatuses, in-a-hurry cautions, simple request section and client care.

Regardless, the time spent in learning the essentials of how to explore stocks and encountering the high points and low points of stock exchanges — regardless of whether there is a greater amount of the last option — is time very much spent, for however long you're relaxing and not risking any cash you can't bear to lose.

CHAPTER FIVE

Contributing is something everybody realizes they ought to do. The securities exchange gives a chance to create financial momentum over the long run, making way for monetary solidness paving the way to and in your brilliant years.

Sadly, putting isn't ordinary in the United States. As per The Ascent, the typical American's reserve funds are just $3,500. Besides, 29% of Americans don't for a moment even have an investment account.

While taking a gander at stock possession in the United States, the numbers are far more terrible. As per a 2020 Gallup survey, some 45% of Americans don't possess a solitary stock!

Quite possibly the main motivation that such countless Americans aren't effective in financial planning is a broadly accepted fantasy that you want a monstrous measure of cash to create a nice yearly return in the securities exchange.

The truth of the matter is that you don't require a lot of cash to create financial well-being. All you truly need is a readiness, to begin with, something and reliably work to build your abundance through little, month-to-month ventures. As a matter of fact, with just $1 each day, you can step making a course toward riches.

The securities exchange has what might be compared to Clark Kent's capacity to fly, a superpower known as intensifying increases. Intensifying increases are benefits that produce more benefits.

Think about it along these lines:

Suppose you make a momentary venture of $100 and, toward the end, you cash in at $110. You saw benefit from your speculation, so you rehash it. Just this time, you have $110 to contribute and accomplish a similar 10% return. By reinvesting your benefits, you exploit intensifying additions, producing $11 in benefits as opposed to $10. Presently, you have a sum of $121 to contribute.

Assuming you were to persistently reinvest your benefits, how much cash made on every single speculation would gradually increment. Throughout quite a while, the distinction consequently will develop to be very significant, although the first speculation sum was never different and the main assets added to the venture were gets back from past speculations.

Most importantly assuming you're searching for establishing a strong financial foundation and valuable open doors, few are very strong accomplished in the securities exchange.

What $1 each Day Turns Into After 30 Years

$1 every day is a modest quantity of cash. To place it into viewpoint, as indicated by Acorns, the typical American burns through $1,100 each year on espresso. That works out to $92 each month, or around $3 each day.

Taking into account that it just expenses $0.27 to make some espresso at home as per Coffee Detective, $1 each day ought not to be difficult to find. You could partake in a couple of cups of espresso consistently if you make it yourself, and assuming that you're similar to the typical American espresso consumer, you reasonable save $2 each day.

While $1 each day isn't a huge load of cash, you wouldn't believe what $1 each day would become in a venture account throughout 30 years. With 365 days in a year, contributing $1 each day for a very long time would bring about a complete head venture of $10,950. In any case, the financial exchange isn't a bank account; it utilizes compound additions as an establishing financial stability strategy.

If you somehow happened to procure a typical yearly return pace of 10%, your $1 each day would develop to become about $57,800 following 30 years. That intends that by putting just $1 each day in the securities exchange, your benefit of $10,950 would be an astounding $46,850. Without a doubt, $46,850 won't construct areas of strength for a record without anyone else, however following an arrangement of beginning little and developing your ventures will.

Put forth Goals to Increase Your Daily Investing Budget by $0.50 each Year

More youthful financial backers commonly have less cash to contribute — that is simply life. At the point when you're youthful, you're tracking down your direction to your vocation and bringing in modest quantities of cash simultaneously. Nonetheless, as you age, you will start to refine your abilities, become more important to your employer — or construct your organization — and start to get more cash flow.

Thus, it's wise to begin little and develop your interests in the securities exchange as your pay fills to create financial wellbeing. An extraordinary technique to do this is to gradually collect how much cash you contribute every day. Consistently, increment the day-to-day speculation sum by $0.50. In the main year, contribute $1 each day, trailed by $1.50 each day in the subsequent year, $2 each day in the third year, $2.50 each day in the fourth year, etc. In doing as such, you will start to construct a significant speculation account.

The Stock Market Is More Small-Fish Friendly Than Ever Before

The times of little savers being compelled to put resources into bank accounts making measly returns even with built revenue are a relic of days gone by. This is to a great extent the consequence of mechanical development making it feasible for little fish to swim in the ocean that is the securities exchange.

A long time back, to contribute, you needed to open an investment fund with a customary dealer, which by and large accompanied robust charges and least equilibrium prerequisites. Nowadays, assuming you need admittance to stocks, trade exchanged reserves (ETFs), shared reserves, or some other monetary resource on the financial exchange, you should simply bounce on the web, and sign in to your number one markdown money market fund, and put in a request.

Eventually, three principal factors have made putting resources into the financial exchange available for the little fish attempting to swim among the sharks:

1. Data Is Available at Your Fingertips

Preceding the accessibility of the present internet-based merchants, on the off chance that you needed admittance to the securities exchange, you needed to acquire it through conventional intermediaries. Today, there are a few choices, including Robinhood, Acorns, Weibull, and a few others that cause effective financial planning conceivable no matter how much cash you have accessible to set aside an underlying instalment into your money market fund.

All you want to do to get to the market is pursue a markdown online intermediary, interface your financial balance, and put aside a little instalment — even as little as $1.

2. Rebate Brokers Make Investing Inexpensive

Conventional merchants accompanied many obstacles. Not in the least did the typical individual not have sufficient cash to open a record, yet commissions on dealers were frequently high to the point that they whittled down any potential benefits the financial backer made.

That is not true anymore.

Today, there's a pattern clearing the web-based rebate specialist industry where dealers are starting to permit financial backers to make without commission exchanges. This implies that when you make an interest in the financial exchange or sell your situation, you just compensate administrative expenses, which work out to be a negligible part of a penny for every offer. Subsequently, the typical financial backer presently approaches individual stocks, file assets, ETFs, and other monetary instruments without paying high commissions that tap into their possible benefits.

3. Partial Shares Give Small Fish Access to Stock Market Shark Food

One more significant issue of the securities exchange of the past was that assuming you believed admittance should exceptionally legitimate organization, you needed to follow through on high per-share costs. For instance, a solitary portion of Amazon.com stock exchanges with a sticker price of above and beyond $3,000 — about how much cash the typical American has in complete reserve funds.

These excessive costs blocked speculations from the typical American, yet all at once, that is all evolving. Nowadays, numerous web-based money market funds empower their financial backers to purchase partial portions of stock. That intends that as opposed to purchasing stock on a for each offer premise, you get it on a dollar-cost premise.

In this way, to purchase $10 worth of Amazon.com stock, you just put in the request and will be given responsibility for a fragmentary portion of the organization upon finishing. Thus, your partial offer will give you openness to the development Amazon.com brings to the table and qualifies you for relative democratic freedoms and profit instalments.

Besides the fact that fragmentary offers permit admittance to stocks that numerous financial backers could not have possibly had, they likewise take into consideration a speculation technique that is based on expansion, no matter how much cash you need to contribute.

Instruments to Help You Start Investing

Since it has become so undeniably obvious how huge of an effect $1 each day can have on your retirement account, you're bound to begin effective money management soon. Nonetheless, putting isn't something you learn in grade school, and many individuals essentially don't have any idea where to begin.

Before making your speculations, it's ideal to investigate as needs be and get a comprehension of how the market functions, contributing methodologies, and how to find actual success as a financial backer, yet that shouldn't prevent you from having the option to watch your total assets develop right away.

There are a few instruments that you can use to get close enough to the market right away and permit the specialists to accept control as you do all necessary investigations. Probably the most ideal choices for fledglings include:

Individual Capital. Individual Capital is a comprehensive individual accounting stage. The stage is intended to assist shoppers with creating financial stability through planning, saving, saving for a secret stash, controlling exorbitant loan costs Visas and different obligations, and exploiting the force of accumulated gains the securities exchange brings to the table.

Improvement. Improvement is a Robo-guide that gives you admittance to the market. The sole objective of the stage is to zero in on money management. You should simply store reserves and the stage will accomplish the work for you with an intensely expanded portfolio including resource classes like ETFs and bonds. While Betterment isn't just robot-counsellor online today, the stage is known for giving a convincing pace of return whether or not you have a truckload of cash, to begin with.

Charles Schwab. Charles Schwab is one of the most confided venture businesses on Wall Street. Albeit the organization offers markdown business administrations, it additionally offers Schwab Intelligent Portfolios, a mechanized, exceptionally enhanced financial planning item similar to Betterments. The significant contrast is that you don't simply get the robot guide with Schwab; you likewise approach human monetary consultants when you want them.

Last Word

The possibility that you must have a huge load of cash to have a significant effect on your future is a legend that keeps numerous away from effective money management to create financial wellbeing, monetary solidness, and an agreeable retirement.

You can begin creating financial well-being and getting ready for your future with just $1 each day. Of course, it's improbable that you'll find your direction to a retirement account with $1 million in it with a $1 each day speculation, however beginning little and developing as your monetary position permits will put you on the way toward independence from the rat race.

As is dependably the situation, when you choose to begin effective financial planning, ensure that you do all necessary investigation and pursue instructed speculation choices.

www.ingramcontent.com/pod-product-compliance
Lightning Source LLC
Chambersburg PA
CBHW070249220526
45465CB00004B/1562